Senior Wonders: People Who Achieved Their Dreams After Age 60

Karen L. Pepkin
Wendell C. Taylor

ISBN: 0615892663
ISBN 13: 9780615892665
Library of Congress Control Number: 2013951336
Karrick Press, Houston, TX

*We gratefully acknowledge Pamela Paradis Metoyer, BA, ELS(D),
for her thoughtful and thorough editing.*

*It's never too late to be what
you might have been.*

\- George Elliot

*What you get by achieving your
goals is not as important as what you
become by achieving your goals.*

\- Henry David Thoreau

Table of Contents

Introduction

Thirty years ago, Karen (one of the authors) decided, at age 33, to move from New York City to Houston, Texas. With no job, family, or friends in Houston, many people thought she was crazy. While in New York, she spoke to her neighbor's friend about her plans. She was pleasantly surprised when the friend said that he thought she was absolutely right in making the move. As a director of a nursing home, the most painful thing he heard from the residents was not regrets about mistakes they made but about things they never tried. They regretted what might have been.

Our book features individuals who, because of their persistence and effort (and luck), first achieved outstanding recognition after age 60. We chose 60 because this age is five years before the traditional retirement age, a time when people reflect on their lives and achievements, and plan what they will do for the next stage of their life.

Baby boomers are now moving into the senior citizen age range. At the same time, life expectancy has increased as a result of better health care, medical advances, and the focus on physical activity and healthy eating. The media abounds with slogans like "60 is the new 40" and "80 is the new 60." Not only are many seniors living longer, but also with more vitality, greater capacity, and renewed energy. So how do we reconcile the remaining years ahead with unfulfilled promises? The answer is you don't have to.

Why do some people want to run a marathon? Why do some people want to climb Mount Everest? Why do some people want to be listed in the *Guinness Book of World Records*? Why do some people continue to strive for personal goals and dreams while others feel that time has passed them by? These questions and others were the inspiration for our book.

In reality, some achievements are age-related such as becoming a ballerina, an ingénue, or winning a gold medal in the 100-yard dash; however, so many other accomplishments are dependent on persistence, effort, ability, opportunity, and luck. Although this book is about those in the 60-plus age-range, the lessons learned from these extraordinary people are universal, whether you are in your 20s, 30s, 40s, 50s, or older. Senior wonders teach us to keep striving and pursuing our goals and dreams and to never give up.

Our book presents 25 brief biographies of people who first accomplished their goals or life-long dreams after reaching the age of 60. For some, it was a personal achievement, like running a marathon; for others it was recognition in their field, like winning an Emmy. We wrote this book to inspire and motivate anyone to continue pursuing personal accomplishments, to not let age be a limiting factor, and to live with no regrets.

Organization of the Book

Individuals selected for our book had to receive national recognition, or accomplish a noteworthy achievement for the first time, after they turned 60 years old. Apart from this common attribute, the "Senior Wonders" selected are a broadly diverse group. Some individuals were in their early 60s when they achieved success, while others were in their 90s when success was first achieved. Senior Wonders included actors, authors, artists, athletes, social activists, and even a Nobel Laureate. They represent women and men, diverse racial and ethnic groups, and nationalities. Furthermore, our Senior Wonders confronted various challenges and obstacles, and with resilience, rose above them.

In researching this book, we found different amounts of information for each of the individuals selected. For some, there was little biographical material available, but we felt their accomplishments merited inclusion in this book. We classified these individuals as "Notables," and included them in a separate section of our book.

Each biography begins with a quote that reflects the person's accomplishment and ends with a quote from the person himself or herself. The web addresses cited at the end of each chapter were current during the time the book was written.

*We know what we are but
not what we may be.*

\- Unknown

Clara Peller

Actress

In her early 80s, Clara Peller became a national celebrity. She appeared on a Wendy's hamburger commercial where she demanded, "Where's the beef?," in a forceful voice, surprising for her diminutive size.

Born: August 4, 1902, in Chicago, Illinois
Died: August 11, 1987

Clara Peller married and had two children. She was widowed in 1982. Peller worked for 35 years as a manicurist and beautician at a Chicago beauty salon. She was discovered at age 80, while still working, by a local ad agency seeking a manicurist for a TV commercial. The commercial was filmed in a Chicago barber shop. The agency later signed her to a contract as an actress because they were impressed by her manners and unique voice.

Peller appeared in numerous regional broadcasts before being signed by the Dancer, Fitzgerald, and Sample Advertising Agency. In 1984, at age 81, Clara Peller was featured in the "Where's the beef?" advertising campaign for the Wendy's fast food restaurant chain. Peller's "Where's the beef?" became a catch phrase across the United States and catapulted the octogenarian into celebrity. The phrase could be seen on tee shirts, coffee mugs, and beach towels. Even former vice president, Walter Mondale, used the phrase, "Where's the beef?" during a debate in his bid to earn the democratic nomination for President of the United States in 1984.

Wendy's sales jumped 31% to $945 million in 1985 and Peller's commercial was credited with the success. A senior vice president for communications at the company, stated "with Clara we accomplished as much in five weeks as we did in 14 ½ years."

Following her success at Wendy's, Clara Peller signed a contract with the Campbell's Soup Company and appeared in an ad for Prego Pasta Plus Spaghetti Sauce. This appearance led to a dispute with Wendy's since in the Campbell's commercial she quipped "I found the beef." Wendy's considered the soup commercial a breach of contract, and in 1985 Peller lost her job with Wendy's.

After starring in these commercials, Peller made the most of her new-found fame, making guest appearances on television, giving press interviews, and appearing in movies. Before her death in 1987, she was inducted in the Advertising Hall of Fame at the Museum of Modern Mythology in San Francisco, California.

In Her Own Words

"I made some money which is nice for an older person, but Wendy's made millions because of me."

Resources

Armstrong, Lois. "Here's the Beef." *People Magazine Online.* People Magazine, 2 April 1984. Web. 15 Dec. 2013.

"Clara Peller, the Actress in 'Where's the Beef?' TV Ad" *New York Times* 12 Aug. 1987. *Gale Biography in Context.* Web 12 Aug 2011.

"Clara Peller-the Actress in Where's the Beef TV Ads." Obituaries. *The New York Times Online.* New York Times, 12 Aug. 1987. Web. 15 Dec. 2013.

"Clara Peller." Newsmakers. Detroit. Gale, 1988. *Gale Biography in Context.* Web 12 Aug 2011

Peller, Clara. "*Wendy's Where's the Beef Commercial.*" YouTube, n.d. Web. 12 Aug 2011.

"Peller, Clara." *Wikipedia.* Wikipedia, 23 Feb. 2008. Web. 15 Dec. 2013. http://en.wikipedia.org/wiki/Clara_Peller

Seger, Linda. *Creating Unforgettable Characters.* New York: Macmillan Press, 1980. Print.

*A diamond is a piece of coal
that stuck to the job.*

- Michael Larsen

Loretta Mary Aiken known as Jackie "Moms" Mabley

Comedian

Mabley was a social commentator and show business pioneer known for her innovative comedy. She paved the way for many future comedians and performers of color, achieving national recognition in her 60s, after nearly 50 years in show business.

Born: March 19, 1894, or 1897, in Brevard, North Carolina
Died: May 23, 1975

Very little is known about the early years of Loretta Mary Aiken. It has been reported, however, that she was a great-granddaughter of a slave. Her father, a grocery store owner, and her mother, had 12 children. Unfortunately her father was killed when she was only a child. For reasons that are unclear, Aiken left home at the age of 13 to join the performers of a traveling minstrel show. In 1913, Aiken began performing with the Theatre Owners Booking Association. She spent her teenage years singing and dancing in black vaudeville on the Chitlin Circuit*. In 1920, after breaking up with her boyfriend, Jack Mabley, she declared, "The least I can do is take his name," so, she changed her name to Jackie Mabley. In 1923, she played in the

Harlem Renaissance theatres and became a favorite. During the following years, she refined her craft and was recognized as a polished comedian among African American audiences.

After age 60, Mabley became a nationally recognized mainstream star. The release of her first album, "The Funniest Woman Alive," by Chess Records in 1960 expanded her popularity. The recording was so popular, it went gold. Her novel stage persona was a toothless woman attired in a house dress and floppy hat. She only had to walk on stage to get a laugh. The theme of her comedy often focused on romantic interests in young men rather than "old geezers." Frequently, she quipped, "There ain't nothing an old man can do for me except bring me a message from a young one."

Mabley became an elite comedian. She recorded more than 20 albums of her comedy routines, appeared in many movies and television shows, and performed at night clubs across the country. In 1962, she played Carnegie Hall. In 1969, she became the oldest person ever to have a United States Top 40 hit. Her version of "Abraham, Martin, and John" reached number 35 on the pop charts. Today, her comedy is remembered as groundbreaking, both for women and African Americans.

*"The '**Chitlin' Circuit**' is the collective name given to the string of performance venues throughout the eastern and southern United States that were safe and acceptable for African American musicians, comedians, and other entertainers to perform in during the age of racial segregation in the United States (from at least the early 19th century through the 1960s) as well as the venues that contemporary African American soul and blues performers, especially in the South, continue to appear at regularly." (Excerpted from Wikipedia 12 August 2011)

In Her Own Words

"I just tell the folks the truth. If they don't want the truth, then don't come to Moms. Anybody that comes to me, I'll help 'em. I don't say anything I don't mean."

Resources

"Jackie 'Moms' Mabley," Contemporary Black Biography. Vol. 15. Detroit: Gale, 1997. *Gale Biography in Context.* Web 12 Aug, 2011.

"Mabley, Jackie Moms." *The African American Registry.* The African American Registry, 2006. Web. 12 Aug 2011. http://www.aaregistry. com/detail.pho?.

"Mabley, Moms." *Encyclopedia Britannica's Guide to Black History Online.* Encyclopedia Britannica, Inc. Web. 12 Aug. 2011. http://www. britannica.com/blackhistory/article-9300767.

"Moms Mabley," St. James Encyclopedia of Popular Culture . Ed. Sara Pendergast and Tom Pendergast. Detroit. St. James Press, 2000. Gale Biography in Context. Web 12 Aug. 2011.

Reimonenq, Alden. "The Harlem Renaissance". *GLBTQ Encyclopedia Online.* GLBTQ Encyclopedia *9 Oct. 2007.* Web. 12 Aug. 2011. <http://www.glbtq.com/literature/harlem/>.

Thompson, M. Cordell. "Moms Mabley Leaves $1/2 Million Estate." *Jet Online.* Jet. 24 July 1975. Web 12 Aug. 2011.

Williams, Elsie A. *The Humor of Jackie "Moms" Mabley: An African American Comedic Tradition.* New York: Garland, 1995. Print.

Success is a result, not a goal.

\- Gustave Flaubert

Margot Gayle

Urban Preservationist and Crusader

In 1970, at age 62, Margot Gayle founded the Friends of Cast Iron Architecture. This organization helped preserve the SoHo district in New York City. She became nationally known as a historic preservationist who was persistent and determined in her efforts to maintain historic landmarks.

Born: May 14, 1908 in Kansas City, Missouri
Died: September 29, 2008

Margot Gayle was born Margot McCoy. Because her father was in the automobile business, the family moved so frequently that she attended a different school every year. Gayle graduated from the University of Michigan and then went to Atlanta where she worked as a social worker while earning a Master of Science degree in bacteriology from Emory University. While in Atlanta, she met and married William T. Gayle, an accountant.

The couple moved to New York City where Gayle worked briefly as a scriptwriter for a television program. She then became a freelance magazine writer, after which she held public relations jobs in city government. In addition to these various positions, she wrote a weekly column on architecture, "New York's Changing Scene," for the New York Daily News Sunday Magazine from 1975 to 1992.

In 1957, she joined The Samuel J. Tilden Club (a democratic reform group) and unsuccessfully ran for City Council. That same year she invited friends to discuss the dysfunctional clocks on the Jefferson Market Courthouse in Greenwich Village. Although the group ostensibly was formed to save the clock, her real purpose was to preserve the building, a Victorian Gothic structure. Because of her efforts, then mayor of New York City, Robert F. Wagner Jr., took the building off the market. The Jefferson Market Courthouse was the first of many such buildings that were saved because of Gayle's work. Her many successes enabled her to enlist the support of such notables as Jane Jacobs (urban planner), Lewis Mumford (influential critic of cities and urban architecture) and ee Cummings (acclaimed poet).

Encouraged by her achievements, Gayle became a strong advocate for landmark preservation laws. New York City passed such a law in 1965. In 1970, at age 62, Gayle formed the Friends of Cast Iron Architecture, which helped defeat the city freeway plan in 1971. Two years later, the twenty-six block Soho neighborhood was designated a historic district. It was this accomplishment for which she received the most recognition. Its Victorian cast iron buildings were preserved.

In addition to her newspaper column, Gayle wrote four books and was active in the Democratic Party. She also started the Victorian Society in America and supported preservation efforts throughout the United States.

In Her Own Words

"Why not let people in the future enjoy some of the things we thought were extremely fine."

Resources

"Margot Gayle: An Oral History Interview." *The New York Preservation Archive Project Online.* The New York Preservation Archive Project, Web. 20 May 2012. <http:www.nypap.org/content/margot-gayle-oral-history-interview/>.

Martin, Douglas. "Margot Gayle, Urban Preservationist and Crusader with Style, dies at 100." New York Times 30 Sept. 2008: B6(L). Gale Biography in Context. Web 12 Aug 2011.

Wood, Anthony C. "Interview with Margot Gale." The New York Preservation Archives Collection. 26 Aug. 1984. Web. 12 Aug. 2011. http://www.nypap.org/content/margot-gayle/.

*A discovery is said to be an accident
meeting a prepared mind.*

- Albert Szent-Gyorgyi

Albert Fert, PhD

Physicist

In 2007, at age 69, Dr. Albert Fert won the Japanese Prize, the Wolf Prize in Physics, and the Nobel Prize. He continues to collaborate and make contributions to the field of spintronics.

Born: March 1938, Carcassone, France

During World War II, Albert Fert lived the life of a country boy, setting snares for rabbits and milking goats. He explored the world of plants and animals, far removed from the world of physics. In June 1945, his father returned from a prisoner of war camp and reunited with his family in Toulouse, France.

Fert's father was a professor at the University of Toulouse and made important contributions to the field of electron microscopy. Fert and his brother became good students, influenced by their father's intellectual discipline. Fert developed a great interest in literature, the arts, and sports. At age 17, he moved to Paris, attracted by the city's diverse intellectual life. He frequented museums, exhibitions, cinemas, concert halls, and jazz clubs and became a passionate fan of jazz, photography, and film. He married Marie-Josee and had two sons, Arian and Bruno.

Fert eventually followed in his father's footsteps, pursuing a career in science. He completed his master's thesis and then pursued his doctorate. When he defended his doctoral thesis in 1970, the technologies available at that time did not permit further advancement of his research. After completing his doctorate in physical sciences, he finished a postdoctoral fellowship at the University of Leeds in England. Deciding to pursue an academic career, he was appointed as assistant professor at the University of Paris-Sud where he supervised a laboratory of doctoral and postdoctoral students. By 1976, he was promoted to professor at the University.

Later in the 1980s, the influence of spin on the mobility of electrons in the atom was fully established. The doctoral work of one of Fert's students confirmed the Spin Hall effects* and it became a hot topic in physics. Fert is credited, along with others, with discovering the phenomenon called giant magnetoresistance (GMR).** He presented his findings to the International Conference of Magnetism, the International Conference of Magnetic Films and Surfaces, and other conferences. He also published his findings in *Physical Review Letters*. His findings provoked considerable interest in the physics community.

The beginning of the 1990s was a productive period for Fert and his research team. The discoveries they made in the 1980s were confirmed by other scientists around the world, thus supporting their important contributions to the science of spintronics.***

In 2007, at age 69, Fert received the Nobel Prize in Physics, the Japanese Prize in physics, and the Wolf Prize in physics. As a result of the Nobel Prize, he received countless requests for speeches. Fert remains enthusiastic about his research and the opportunities to develop new ideas in his field. Despite his remarkable accomplishments, Fert credits his successes to productive collaborations with bright students and colleagues.

*The Spin Hall effect is a phenomenon of inducing spin current by an external electric field.

**Giant magnetoresistance is a large change in resistance (typically 10 to 20%) when the devices are subjected to a magnetic field, compared with a maximum sensitivity of a few percent for other types of magnetic sensors.

***Spintronics is also known as magnetoelectronics, an emerging technology exploiting both the intrinsic spin of the electron and its associated magnetic moment, in addition to its fundamental electronic charge, in solid-state devices.

Resources
"Albert Fert-Biographical." *Nobelprize.org.* Nobel Media AB 2013. Web. 5 Nov 2012.

http://nobelprize.org/nobel_prizes/Physics/laureates/2007/fert.bio.html/.

Grandin, Karl, ed. *The Nobel Prizes 2007.* Nobel Foundation: Stockholm, 2008. Print.

NVE Corporation. Web. 4 Nov. 2012. http://www.gmrsensors.com/gmr-operation.htm/.

"Spin Hall Effects." *Microsoft Academic Search.* Web. 4 Nov. 2012.

http://academic.research.microsoft.com/Keyword/69260/Spin-Hall-Effect

Just when the caterpillar thought the world was over, it became a butterfly.-

- Proverb

Harry Bernstein

Author

Harry Bernstein's career was devoted to writing. He achieved literary success at age 97 by publishing the first of three biographical novels in 2007. In 2008, at age 98, he was awarded a Guggenheim Fellowship to support his writing.

Born: April 17 or May 30, 1910, in Stockport, England
Died: June 3, 2011

Harry Bernstein began writing when a teacher at his technical school discouraged him from becoming an architect. He moved to New York and published stories in several magazines, but did not achieve the success he had hoped for. He married Ruby in 1935 and they had two children.

In the 1950s, Bernstein tried to make a living as a freelance journalist and a scriptwriter for Columbia Pictures, but was barely able to make ends meet. Ruby had to subsidize his income as a school secretary. During his career, Bernstein worked for various movie production companies and as a magazine editor for trade magazines. He also wrote freelance articles for publications such as *Newsweek*, *Popular Mechanics*, and the *Jewish American Monthly*. He retired in 1971 at age

62. In 1981, Bernstein published a novel, *The Smile*, which was unsuccessful. Undaunted, he continued to write, penning more than 20 other unpublished novels.

When Ruby died in 2002, after 67 years of marriage, Bernstein picked up his pen again, writing *The Invisible Wall* about an "invisible wall" that separated the Jewish section of the mill town from the Christian section. Published in 2007, when Bernstein was 97, it described his poverty-stricken upbringing in a small English mill town, and his parents' emigration from Poland. The book also described how Bernstein's father, a dictatorial bully, emotionally brutalized his wife and seven children. He brought to life his childhood experiences with anti-Semitism, and his sister's forbidden romance with a Christian lover.

At age 98, in 2008, Bernstein's second book, *The Dream*, was published. This book centered on his family's move to Chicago in 1922 when he was 12 and his family's relationship during the difficult years of the Great Depression. Bernstein's novels were received with such critical acclaim, that in 2008 he was awarded a *Guggenheim Fellowship*, to further pursue his writing. His third book, *The Golden Willow: The Story of a Lifetime of Love*, was published at age 99, in 2009. This book described his married life and later years. His novels have been translated and published in Sweden, Germany, Finland, Norway, Denmark, and Brazil.

In His Own Words

"I was too much alone. My wife was dead. My friends were mostly gone. I had no future to think about, no present and so I found myself thinking about my past, and the people I knew and the place I grew up. I was looking for a home."

"If I had not lived until I was 90, I would not have been able to write this book…It could not have been done even when I was 10 years younger. I wasn't ready. God knows what other potentials lurk in other people, if we could only keep them alive well into their 90s."

Resources

Grimes, William. "Harry Bernstein, Late Blooming Author, Dies at 101." New York Times 7 June 2011: A 29 (L) *Gale Biography in Context.* Web. 12 Aug. 2011.

"Harry Bernstein." Contemporary Authors on Line. Detroit: Gale, 2011. *Gale Biography in Context.* Web. 12 Aug. 2011.

Rich, Motoko. "Successful at 96, Writer Has More to Say." The New York Times. The New York Times, 7 April 2007. Web. 10 Nov. 2012.

Overcome the notion that you must be regular. It robs you of the chance to be extraordinary.

- Unknown

Clementine Hunter

Artist

Clementine Hunter was a gifted folk artist who began painting in her 50s. Her work helped preserve the cultural and historical activities of Southern plantation life from the African American perspective. She received national recognition for her work, which is now part of 20 permanent collections across the United States.

Born: December 19, 1886 (or January 1887), in Cloutierville, Louisiana

Died: January 1, 1988

Clementine Hunter was born Clemence Reuben, later changing her name to Clementine. She briefly attended a small Catholic school but remained illiterate all of her life. When Hunter was eight years old, her family moved to the Melrose Plantation in Natchitoches, Louisiana. She lived with Charlie Dupree and the couple had a boy and a girl. Charlie died in 1914. In 1924, she married Emanuel Hunter, and they had five children.

Clementine Hunter worked as a domestic and a field hand from the 1900s to the late 1920s. During this time, she created quilts, baskets, and high tide lace, and engaged in other handicrafts. These passions continued throughout her life. She also earned a reputation as a creative cook.

In 1939, at age 51, Hunter began to paint. Using leftover paints from a visiting artist, she completed her first painting and showed it to Frances Mignon. Mignon, a resident of Melrose Plantation who later became the curator of its art collection, had a strong influence on her artistic career. He recognized her talent and, with his support, she began to paint on any surface she found. She used bottles, old iron pots, paper bags, cardboard boxes, gourds, scraps of wood, and many other objects. She began by painting afterhours, frequently painting late into the night while continuing to create her quilts. Hunter painted from her memories or from dreams rather than from real life. Typically, her subjects focused on work, religion, and play.

James Register, another visitor to Melrose Plantation, was a writer, artist, and teacher at the University of Oklahoma. After seeing Hunter's work, he also supported and encouraged her by sending supplies and cash payments and assisting her in obtaining a foundation grant.

Hunter experimented with other art forms. In her late 60s, she painted a mural. In her 70s, she painted a series of pictures that were influenced by montages- art work created by assembling small pieces of different materials. Although Hunter returned to her primitive style, montages continued to influence her paintings.

In 1955, the New Orleans Museum of Art gave Hunter (in her 70s) her first solo exhibition, the first offered to an African American artist. In 1956, she created some of her most important works- the African House Murals at Melrose. These murals of Louisiana gave a view of plantation life along the Cane River. At the same time Northwestern State College in Louisiana, held its first "all Hunter show."

During her lifetime, Clementine Hunter had more than 20 solo exhibitions at galleries, museums, and universities. She was invited to the White House by President Jimmy Carter and received an honorary doctorate from Northwestern State College in 1986. She remains, as a Look Magazine art critic once proclaimed, "among the most notable primitive painters in the country."

In Her Own Words

"Soon as I light my lamp, a whole lot of things goin' cross my mind and 'fore I know it, I'm gettin' em' down on paper."

"I don't pass for knowing about painting. Other folks say they get training and paint by rules. I can't paint my pictures by rule. I paint them by heart."

Resources

"Clementine Hunter. " *Contemporary Black Biography* Vol 45. Detroit: Gale 2004. *Gale Biography in Context.* Web. 12 Aug. 2011.

"Clementine Hunter" *Notable Black American Women.* Gale 1992. *Gale Biography in Context.* Web. 12 Aug. 2011.

"Clementine Hunter." *St. James Guide to Black Artists.* Gale, 1997. *Gale Biography in Context.* Web. 12 Aug. 2011.

Lyons, Mary E., ed. *Talking with Tebé: Clementine Hunter, Memory Artist.* Boston: Houghton Mifflin, 1998. Print.

Success is as much a matter of luck as of ability, but perhaps even more, of persistence, 'sticking it' until luck turns.

\- B. H. Liddell

Estelle Getty (Estelle Scher Gettleman)

Actor

After working many years as an actress, Estelle Getty landed the role of her lifetime at age 62 - playing the sarcastic Sophia Petrillo on the television show, the Golden Girls. After this success, she was featured in other television shows and in movies.

Born: July 25, 1923, in New York City
Died: July 22, 2008

Estelle Getty, born Estelle Scher to immigrant Polish parents, was raised in New York City. She later changed her name to Estelle Getty. At age four, she fell in love with the theater when her parents took her to a Vaudeville show. Although her family supported her desire to be in show business, her father insisted that she learn office skills to be able to support herself. Getty got her start in Yiddish theater and as a stand-up comedian in the "Borscht Belt"* (Catskill Mountains). She wasn't particularly successful there, but it was during this time that she developed her trademark one-line zingers.

In 1947, Getty married Arthur Gettleman and they had two sons. She worked in office jobs to help support her family as she continued to strive for success as an actress. Getty got her first significant role in 1970 in the off-Broadway play, "Torch Song Trilogy" playing an ill-natured mother. For 40 years, she worked in relative obscurity before she landed the part of Sophia Petrillo, the sarcastic octogenarian on *The Golden Girls*, when she was 62. Ironically, the producers weren't sure she was old enough for the part and had her audition multiple times before giving her the role.

The Golden Girls was an immediate hit, partly because of Sophia's verbal zingers. Getty continued in that role for the duration of the show (from 1985 to 1992). Although Sophia originally was a minor role, Getty's interpretation of the character led to its increased popularity, and to story lines that allowed a more substantial interplay with the show's other characters. In 1986, at age 63, Getty won a Golden Globe award for her portrayal of Sophia. From 1986 to 1992, she was nominated for an Emmy award for outstanding supporting actress in a comedy series, winning in 1988, at age 65.

During *The Golden Girls*, other roles came her way. She had a small role in the films *Tootsie, Deadly Force, and Victims for Victims-The Theresa Saldano Story.* She was Cher's mother in *Mask,* Sylvester Stallone's mother in *Stop or My Mother Will Shoot,* and had a small part in Barry Manilow's television movie *Copacabana.* From 1993 to 1995, Getty was featured on the television program *The Empty Nest.* Altogether, she appeared in 180 episodes of *The Golden Girls, Empty Nest, Golden Palace, Nurses,* and *Blossom.*

At age 65, Getty co-wrote her autobiography titled, *If I Knew Then, What I Know Now...So What?* At age 70, she released an exercise video for senior citizens. Getty was also an outspoken supporter of gay rights and an active fund raiser for AIDS research. After Getty's death, fans voted for their favorite episode of *The Golden Girls* featuring Sophia. The episode titled "Old Friends" received the most votes.

*Borscht Belt, or Jewish Alps, is a colloquial term for the mostly defunct summer resorts of the Catskill Mountains in parts of Sullivan,

Orange and Ulster counties in upstate New York that were a popular vacation spot for New York City Jews from the 1920s up to the 1970s.

In Her Own Words

"To you this is just a job. To me it's my entire career down the toilet unless you make me look 80."

"I knew I could be seduced by success in another field so I said, 'Don't promote me please.'"

Resources

"Estelle Getty." *Wikipedia*. Wikipedia, Web. 4 Nov. 2012. http://en.wikipedia.org/wiki/Borscht_Belt.

"Getty Dies at 84." *Yahoo Entertainment Report*. Yahoo Entertainment Report, July 2008, Web. 10 Nov. 2012.

Getty, Estelle, and Steve Delsohn. *If I Knew Then What I Know Now...So What?* New York: McGraw Hill/Contemporary, 1989. Print.

"Getty Found 'Golden' success later in life." Variety 28 July 2008: 40. Gale Biography in Context. Web 12 Aug. 2011.

"Golden Girl Estelle Getty Dead at 84." KTLA. KTLA, 22 July 2008. Web. 10 Nov. 2012. http://ktla.trb.com/news/ktla-estelle-getty.0.story

"Obituaries" *Hollywood Reporter* 23 July 2008: 17. *Gale Biography in Context*. Web.12 Aug. 2011.

Thomas, Bob. "ESTELLE GETTY: 84." Globe & Mail [Toronto, Canada] 23 July 2008 S10. *Gale Biography in Context* Web. 12 Aug 2011. Web. 10 Nov. 2012. http://www.EstelleGetty.com .

*Once we believe in ourselves, we can
risk curiosity, wonder, spontaneous
delight, or any experience that
reveals the human spirit.*

- e.e. Cummings.

Harriet Doerr

Novelist

Harriet Doerr, at age 73, wrote her first novel, Stones for Ibarra, *which received critical acclaim and won the American Book Award for first fiction as well as many other awards.* Stones for Ibarra *was described by another author as "the perfect book."*

Born: April 8, 1910, in Pasadena, California
Died: November 24, 2002

Harriet Doerr was born Harriet Green Huntington, in Pasadena, California, the third of six children. She was a daughter of a California railroad magnate and grew up in a family that encouraged intellectual endeavors. Doerr was asked to read her poetry at her high school graduation, but she declined to have the school publish the poems because she thought they were not good enough.

In 1927, Harriet Doerr attended Smith College in Northampton, Massachusetts, but returned to California because she didn't like the cold and wanted to be with her boyfriend, Albert Doerr. She transferred to Stanford University, to be close to him, but left college to marry him. They had two children, a son and a daughter.

Albert Doerr's family owned a copper mine in the Mexican state of Aguascaliente, and the time she spent in this setting provided the subject matter for her later writing. Her husband was diagnosed with leukemia and struggled with the disease until his death in 1972. After his death, Doerr returned to California and resumed her education. From 1975 to 1976, she took writing courses at Scripps College. In 1977, Doerr re-enrolled in Stanford University as a history major and was later accepted into the university's creative writing program. In 1979, Doerr earned a Stegner Fellowship and began publishing short stories.

In 1982, at age 72, Doerr won the Transatlantic Review–Henfield Foundation Award for three stories she had published in small literary magazines. Her stories came to the attention of Viking's senior editors who suggested that she combine her short stories into a novel. In 1984, at age 74, Doerr published *Stones for Ibarra* and won that year's National Book Award for a first book of fiction. This book was highly acclaimed, and a television adaptation of *Stones for Ibarra* was presented by the Hallmark Hall of Fame, in 1988.

Harriet Doerr was passionate about her writing. In 1990, she wrote a collection of stories, *Under the Aztec Sun* (Yolla Bolly Press, Covelo, California). In 1993, at 83, she published her second novel, *Consider This Senora* (Harcourt, New York). In 1995, Doerr published a collection of short stories and essays, *The Tiger in the Grass: Stories and Other Inventions* (Viking, New York). Some of these stories were personal and described her son's battle with cancer, a disease that also killed her parents, husband, and five of her siblings. She also contributed to anthologies, including *The Writer of Her Work* (1991) and *The Best American Short Stories* (1989) and periodicals, including *The New Yorker*, *Los Angeles Times Magazine*, the *Santa Monica Review*, the *Atlantic Monthly*, and *Epoch*. She won numerous awards for this writing.

In 2002, Doerr died, at age 92, from complications of a broken hip.

In Her Own Words

"At this age you don't delay. You simply don't get more and more energy as time passes. It doesn't mean you are going out of your mind, but that finding the words you are looking for doesn't happen as quickly."

Resources

"Harriet Doerr." *Contemporary Authors Online.* Detroit: Gale, 2003. *Gale Biography in Context.* Web 12 Aug. 2011.

Martin, Douglas. "Harriet Doerr is dead at 92; Writer of searing, sparse prose." New York Times 27 Nov. 2002: C1 Gale Biography in Context. Web. 12 Aug. 2011.

*The person who makes a success
of living is the one who sees
his goal steadily and aims for it
unswervingly. That is dedication.*

- Cecil B. Demille

Jacques Henri Lartigue

Photographer/Painter

After limited success as a painter, Jacques Henri Lartigue found his true calling in photojournalism in his 60s and is now considered one of the greatest photodiarists of his time.

Born: June 13, 1894, in Courbevoie, France
Died: September 12, 1986

Jacques Henri Lartigue learned about photography from his father early in his life. His father, Henri Lartigue, bought him his first camera when he was eight years old. This camera enabled Lartigue to provide an ongoing record of his childhood, which included automobile outings, family holidays, and especially his older brother Maurice's inventions. Both brothers were fascinated by cars, aviation, and sports. Lartigue's camera froze each moment in time. Because of the belief that a snapshot cannot encompass all there is to say and to remember about life, Lartigue began keeping a journal and continued to do so his entire life. He also took up drawing and painting. In 1915, he briefly attended the Julian Academy where painting became his main profession. Beginning in 1922, he exhibited his work in shows in Paris and in the south of France.

In 1919, Lartigue married Madeleine Messager. Their son Dani was born in 1921, and in 1931 the couple divorced. The decline of Lartigue's family fortunes forced him to search for other sources of income. He refused, however, to take a steady job and lose his freedom; so he existed on a limited income by selling his paintings during the 1930s and 1940s. At the beginning of the 1950s, his work as a photographer was noticed; nevertheless, he continued to paint. Painting was his profession, and he achieved some success with exhibits in French salons.

Lartigue and his third wife, Florette, took a cargo ship to Los Angeles in 1962. They stopped on the East Coast and met Charles Rado of the Rapho Agency. Rado in turn contacted John Szwarkoski, a young curator in the photography department at the Museum of Modern Art in New York. Lartigue's photography exhibit was well received at the museum. In 1963, the museum presented a selection of the many photographs he had taken throughout his life. In the same year, a photographic spread of his work was featured in the famous *Life Magazine* issue that commemorated the death of President John Fitzgerald Kennedy and was publicized worldwide. This photographic spread launched Lartigue's career as a photographer at age 69. Three years later, with his first book, *The Family Album*, he achieved worldwide fame and established his reputation as a photographer.

Lartigue had many achievements. In 1970, at age 76, he wrote *The Diary of a Century*. In 1974, he was commissioned by the President of France, Valéry Giscard d'Estaing, to shoot an official portrait photograph. In 1975, the first retrospective of Lartigue's work was held in the Musée des Arts Décoratifs in Paris. In 1979, Lartigue signed a donation agreement and became the first living French photographer to donate his work to the nation. He also authorized the Association des Amis de Jacques Henri Lartigue to preserve and promote the collection. In 1980, at age 86, his dream of having his own museum came true with the exhibit "Bonjour Monsieur Lartigue," at the Grand Palais.

He continued his work as a photographer, painter, and writer until his death at age 92 in Nice, France on September 12, 1986. His legacy includes more than 100,000 snapshots, 7,000 diary pages and 1,500 paintings.

Resources

"Jacques Henri Lartigue." Contemporary Authors on Line. Detroit. Gale. 2003. Gale Biography in Context. Web 12 Aug 2011.

Jacques Henri Lartigue Pics. Web. 30 Nov. 2013. http://www.whosdatedwho.com/celebrities/people/dating/jacques-henri-lartigue.htm/.

Johnson, Ken. "Jacques Henri Lartigue. Imprints of Joy." New York Times 20 Oct. 2000 E40. Gale Biography in Context. Web 12 Aug 2011.

Schwabsky, Barry. "Jacques Henri Lartigue. Hayward Gallery." Artforum International 43.3 (2004) 237+ Gale Biography in Context. Web. 12 Aug 2011.

Web. 16 Feb. 2010. http://www.lartigue.org/us2/jhlartigue/jhlp-bio.html/. http://www.lartigue.org/us2/jhlartigue/index.html/.

Never, never, never, give up.

\- Winston Churchill

Nola Ochs

Oldest College Graduate

Nola Ochs has the distinction of being the oldest person to graduate from college. She completed her bachelors' degree in 2007, at age 95, a master's degree in 2010, at age 98. She has inspired people of all ages to achieve their goals and realize that learning is a lifelong pursuit.

Born: 1911 in Hays, Kansas

Nola Ochs was born in 1911 in Hays, Kansas. Her mother and her paternal grandfather were teachers. Ochs credits her family with her love of learning. She graduated from high school in 1929 and began college in April 1930 with a correspondence course from Fort Hays State University in Kansas. She passed her teacher's certification exam and taught in county high schools for four years. Soon after, she married her husband Vernon Ochs. They lived together on a farm until Vernon's death at age 61 in 1972. The couple raised their four sons; she now has 13 grandchildren and 15 great grandchildren.

As a farmer's wife and mother, Ochs deferred her educational goals but always had a thirst for knowledge. After her husband died, she considered returning to school. In 1978, at age 67, she enrolled in Dodge City Community College and took a tennis class. Her charm and down-to-earth attitude helped her easily fit in with the younger students. Enrolling first in an agribusiness marketing class, over the next 10 years Ochs eventually completed classes that interested her. She particularly enjoyed history and English. A professor reviewed her transcript and told her that she could graduate with an associate's degree, if she completed a college algebra course. Ochs passed the required class and soon graduated.

Inspired by her accomplishments, Ochs decided to pursue a four-year degree. She contacted Fort Hays State University, where she had been a student in the 1930s. After an extensive investigation, an academic advisor found documentation of the credits she had earned. Ochs needed another 30 credits to complete a bachelor's degree.

Initially, Ochs traveled 100 miles to the university to take classes, but eventually decided to move from her farm to live in an apartment nearby the campus. In 2007, at age 95, Ochs graduated with a 3.7 grade-point average, setting a record as the world's oldest college graduate. She continued her graduate education at the same university and received a master's degree in liberal arts with a concentration in history, in 2010, at age 98. Ochs has received mail from all over the world praising her for her accomplishments and acknowledging her as an inspiration for others.

In Her Own Words

"…You know, people retire. That doesn't mean to sit down and stay there or watch TV. Retirement ought to give us time to go out and just do what we want to do. So my advice is to satisfy some desire that we have within ourselves to get out, to go see people, travel a little, anything that they'd like to do rather than just be idle."

Resources

"Nola Ochs, 98 Years Old, to Get Master's Degree." *Huffington Post Online.* Huffington Post. 11 May 2010. Web. 30 Nov. 2013.

"Woman, 95, Set to Be Oldest College Graduate." Wonderful World on NBC News.com. NBC News, 27 April 2007. Web. 30 Nov. 2013.

"World's Oldest Bachelor's Graduate Finishing Up Graduate Work on FHSU Campus." *Fort Hays State University Online.* Fort Hays State University. Web. 30 Nov. 2013.

You are old when you have
more regrets than dreams.

- Unknown

Barbara Hillary

Adventurer, Community Activist

Reaching the North Pole poses tremendous physical, psychological, financial, and climatic challenges. In 2006, at age 75, Barbara Hillary became the first African American woman to overcome these formidable challenges and reach the North and South Poles.

Born: June 12, 1931, in New York City

Barbara Hillary grew up in Harlem. Her father died when she was a baby and to support the family, her mother worked as a domestic. During this time, Hillary read many books about extreme challenges and human endurance.

Hillary earned both bachelor's and master's degrees majoring in gerontology. Working as a nurse, she helped sensitize staff to the needs of their clients by making the staff aware of their own aging process. After many years of dedicated service, she retired from the nursing profession.

At age 67, Hillary battled lung cancer and later breast cancer and survived. After this life-changing experience, she became interested in nontraditional adventurous vacations.

Hillary took her first trip abroad, alone, to Guyana in 1992. Five years later, she went dog-sledding in Quebec and photographed polar bears in Manitoba. When Hillary learned that an African American woman had never reached the North Pole, she decided to undertake the challenge.

To prepare for her Arctic adventure, she took lessons in cross-country skiing and hired a personal trainer so she could develop the physical fitness needed for the trip. The training itself was demanding because she had never skied before and had to have the strength to pull a sled on skis, and be able to drive a snow mobile.

Physical fitness was not the only challenge. When Hillary researched the costs of the trip, she found that Eagle's Cry Adventures took people to the North Pole for $16,000. Her savings were inadequate, so she had to solicit thousands of dollars in donations. Midway through her fitness training, the price of the trip was raised to $21,000 because of currency fluctuations and other factors. Hillary then had to raise additional funds. After she was featured in an article in The New Yorker, several weeks before her departure, she received enough contributions to make the trip.

Barbara Hillary arrived in Longyearbyen, Norway, on April 18, 2007. After passing the required fitness test, she was flown to Base Camp Barneo, on an ice floe 60 miles from the North Pole. She and her fellow travelers pitched their tents and on April 23, Hillary and two trained guides set off on their trip. Days later, she reached the North Pole, becoming the first known African American woman, and one of the oldest people at age 75, to accomplish this feat. In 2011, at age 80, she journeyed to the South Pole and became the first African American woman to reach both poles.

Hillary is committed to fighting global warming at a grass-roots level and advocating for her community. She is the founder and editor-in-chief of *The Peninsula Magazine* in Queens, New York, a non-profit and community focused publication.

Barbara Hillary has received many awards for her accomplishments. She received the Spirit of America award from the National Recreational Vehicle Association and the Individual of Inspiration and Dedication award from the Office of the Borough President of Brooklyn, New York. In addition, a resolution honoring and recognizing her achievement was introduced in the United States House of Representatives.

In Her Own Words

"I always had dreams of travel, but much of travel, as I saw it, was so sheep-like, so John Doe."

"…[I]f I am going to die, I want to go doing something I enjoy."

Resources

"Barbara Hillary," *Contemporary Black Biography*. Vol. 65. Detroit: Gale, 2008. *Gale Biography in Context*. Web. 12 Aug. 2011.

Collins, Lauren. "TRUE NORTH," The New Yorker 26 Mar. 2007: 32. Gale Biography in Context. Web. 12 Aug. 2011.

"Hillary, Barbara." BarbaraHillary.com, 2009. Web. 30 Nov. 2013. http://BarbaraHillary.com.

Hoffman, Melody K. "Barbara Hillary skis into history as first Black woman to reach North Pole." *Jet* 28 May 2007: 36. *Gale Biography in Context*. Web. 12 Aug. 2011.

Of all the forces that make for a better world, none is so powerful as hope. With hope, one can think, one can work, one can dream. If you have hope, you have everything.

- Anonymous

Laura Ingalls Wilder (Born Laura Elizabeth Ingalls)

Author

While in her 60s, as a result of her daughter's encouragement, Wilder cre-ated a series, The Little House Books, *which recounted her childhood on the American frontier in the mid-to-late 1800s. Her books are considered children's classics. These books became very popular with adults and children and were later made into a long-running television series,* Little House on the Prairie.

Born: February 7, 1867, in Pepin, Wisconsin
Died: February 10, 1957

Laura Ingalls Wilder (born Laura Elizabeth Ingalls) grew up in a family very much like the family later depicted in her books. Her family included father Charles, mother Caroline, and sisters Grace, Carrie, and Mary. Her brother, Charles Jr., died in infancy. During her childhood, her family moved frequently to find better opportunities.

Wilder became a school teacher and taught in DeSmet, in the Dakota Territory (now South Dakota) from 1882 to1885. In 1885, at age 28, she quit her teaching position to marry Almonzo James Wilder. The couple earned their living as farmers near DeSmet moving briefly to Florida to recover from illnesses. During their marriage, the Wilders faced many challenges. In 1889, a son died during childbirth. Soon after, Almonzo contracted diphtheria which left him partially paralyzed. In the same year, their house burned to the ground.

The Wilder family overcame these tragedies and continued to farm their land. In 1917, Laura Ingalls Wilder helped organize the Mansfield Farm Loan Association and served as its secretary and treasurer.

Although Wilder wrote her first article, for the *Missouri Realist,* titled "Favors the Small Farm" in 1911, she did not become a serious writer until her 60s. Her daughter encouraged her to record her vivid memories of her childhood in the pioneer Midwest and offered to edit her mother's writing. Rather than write a biography, Wilder wrote a series of short books that read like fiction. In 1932, at age 65, she published the first of her books, *Little House in the Big Woods,* followed by, *The Long Winter* in 1940, *Little Town on the Prairie* in 1941, and *These Happy Golden Years* in 1943. She wrote the last book in the Little House series in 1943 at age 76.

Wilder received many awards for her writing. In 1938 and 1939, she won the Newberry Honor Book Award for *On the Banks of Plum Creek* and for *By the Shores of Silver Lake.* In 1942, she received the Pacific Northwest Library Association Young Readers' Choice Award for *By the Shores of Silver Lake.* In 1943, she was awarded the Book World Children's Spring Book Festival Award for *These Happy Golden Years.*

Wilder's books quickly became classics. They have been continuously in print since their initial publication and have been translated into 40 different languages. In addition, The Little House book series has spawned a multimillion dollar franchise of mass marketing, spinoff book series, and a long running television show, "Little House on the Prairie," that starred Michael Landon. In total, she published nine children's books and six books for adults about her philosophy of personal freedom and liberty as well as other topics.

To honor Wilder's writing success, in 1951, a library was named after her in Mansfield, Missouri. In 1954, the American Library Association established the Laura Ingalls Wilder Medal to honor an author or illustrator who has contributed to children's literature over a period of years. Wilder was the first recipient of this medal. After her death in 1957, Wilder was elected to the Ozark Hall of Fame. In 1978, she was inducted into the South Dakota Cowboy Western Hall of Fame.

In Her Own Words

"I realized that I had seen and lived it all.... I wanted children now to understand more about the beginning of things, to know what is behind the things they see—and what it is that made America as they know it...."

Resources

Anderson, William. *Laura Ingalls Wilder: A Biography.* New York: HarperCollins, 1992. Print.

"Laura (Elizabeth) Ingalls Wilder." St. James Guide to Children's Writers. 1999 *Gale Biography in Context.* Web. 12 Aug. 2011.

"Laura Ingalls Wilder Encyclopedia World Biography, Vol. 18, Detroit: Gale, 1998. Gale Biography in Context. Web. 12 Aug. 2011.

MacBride, RL, ed. *West From Home: Letters of Laura Ingalls Wilder to Almanzo.* New York: Harper, 1974. Print.

Miller, John E. *Becoming Laura Ingalls Wilder: the Woman Behind the Legacy.* Columbia: University of Missouri Press, 1998. Print.

Spaeth, Janet. *Laura Ingalls Wilder. Boston:* Twayne P, 1987. Print.

Vedder, Pauli A. "Laura (Elizabeth) Ingalls Wilder." Contemporary Authors on Line. Detroit: Gale, 2003. Gale Biography in Context. Web. 12 Aug. 2011.

Wadsworth, Ginger. *Laura Ingalls Wilder: Storyteller of the Prairie.* Minneapolis: Lerner, 1997. Print.

Web. 20 May 2012. http://lauralittlehouseontheprairie.blogspot.com/2008/04/laura-ingalls-wilder-timeline.html/

Web. 12 Aug. 2011. www.notablebiographies.com/We-Z/Wilder-Laura-Ingalls.html/

Zochert, Donald. *Laura: The Life of Laura Ingalls Wilder.* Chicago: Regnery, 1976. Print.

Believe in yourself and all that you are.
Know that there is something inside
yourself that is greater than any obstacle.

- Christian D. Larsen

Frank McCourt

Author

Because of limited job opportunities, Frank McCourt's family left New York City to return to his parents' native Ireland where they continued to endure unending poverty. Through ingenuity and persistence, McCourt found his way back to the city and became a teacher. After retiring, he wrote Angela's Ashes, *a memoire of his childhood for which he garnered national acclaim and a Pulitzer Prize.*

Born: August 19, 1930 in Brooklyn, New York
Died: July 19, 2009

Frank (born Frances) McCourt, the son of Malachi and Angela McCourt, was born in Brooklyn, New York. Because of the Great Depression, he and his family returned to their mother's native Limerick, Ireland, in 1934. Unfortunately, their hopes of improving their economic situation did not materialize and in fact worsened. His father would work hard during the week and drink away his earnings on the weekend. The family lived in a tiny cottage next to an outhouse that frequently flooded their home with sewage. The family was so poor, they all shared a single flea-ridden bed. If the unending poverty wasn't enough, the family had to battle ethnic prejudice because his father was a northern Irishman.

When McCourt was age 14, his father abandoned the family for a job in England and only occasionally returned after spending all his earnings on alcohol. Despite being considered a gifted student, McCourt dropped out of school to work at menial jobs to help support his family.

At age 19, he left Ireland, having saved enough money for passage on a ship to America. Shortly after his arrival, he was drafted into the Korean War. When he returned from the war, McCourt took advantage of the GI Bill. Because he had never attended high school but was well read, he "talked his way into" acceptance into New York University and graduated with a bachelor's degree in 1957. He continued his education at Brooklyn College and, in 1967, received a master's degree.

After graduating from New York University, McCourt became an English teacher in the New York City school system. He first taught at a vocational/technical school on Staten Island where he earned an excellent reputation as a tough teacher. This reputation led to his next position at the prestigious Stuyvesant High School. After 30 years, he retired from the New York City school system.

During his years as a teacher, McCourt would always tell his students, "Write what you know." In 1984, he took his own advice. He and his brother wrote and acted in a review of their life experiences, *A Couple of Blaguards*.

In 1994, Frank McCourt decided to write his autobiography. Named for his mother, *Angela's Ashes* was published when McCourt was age 66. It describes McCourt's impoverished childhood in Ireland. Part of the appeal of the book was McCourt's ability to turn what should be horrific memories into amusing anecdotes. In 1997, the book won a Pulitzer Prize, the *Los Angeles Times* Book Award, and the *New York Times* Editor's Choice Distinction. *Angela's Ashes* was so successful it was made into a movie in 1999.

McCourt continued to have success as a writer. In 1998, his play *The Irish…How They Got That Way*, had a successful run. In 1999, he published *Tis, a Memoir*, which focused on his life as a new immigrant in America. McCourt was awarded the Action Against Hunger Humanitarian Award in 2002 for bringing an honest portrayal of hunger to a mass audience. McCourt collaborated with Action Against Hunger for a decade in his capacity as advisor, and even hosted a video chronicling its work in the field. In 2005, he published *Teacher Man*, which described the challenges of being a young inexperienced teacher.

In His Own Words

"I couldn't have written this book fifteen years ago because I was carrying a lot of baggage around…and I had attitudes… these attitudes had to be softened. I had to get rid of them; I had to become, as it says in the Bible, as a child. The child started to speak in this book. And that was the only way to do it, without judging."

Resources

"Action Against Hunger Mourns Loss of Author & Humanitarian Frank McCourt." Action Against Hunger. Action Against Hunger, 22 July 2009. Web. 4 Nov. 2012.

"'Angela's Ashes' Author Frank McCourt Has Cancer." *USA Today Online*. USA Today, 20 May 2009. Web. 30 Nov. 2013.

"Frank McCourt," Authors and Artists for Young Adults: Vol 61. Gale, 2005. Gale Biography in Context. Web 12 Aug. 11.

"Frank McCourt," *Contemporary Authors Online*. Detroit: Gale, 2009. *Gale Biography in Context*. Web. 12 Aug 2011.

"Frank McCourt," *Newsmakers*. Detroit: Gale, 1997 *Gale Biography in Context*. Web. 12 Aug 2011.

Grimes, William. "Frank McCourt, Author of Angela's Ashes, Dies at 78." New York Times. New York Times, 19 July 2009. Web. 30 Nov. 2013.

Web. 4 Nov. 2012. http://www.actionagainsthunger.org/blog/action-against-hunger-mourns-loss-author-humanitarian-frank-mccourt/.

If it is to be, it is up to me.

- William H. Johnson

Maggie Kuhn

Social Activist

In 1970, at age 65, Maggie Kuhn founded the Gray Panthers, an organization devoted to eliminating forced retirement, promoting nursing home reform, and combating health-care fraud. Her organization was part of a new movement that fought against ageism, racism, sexism, and militarism.

Born: August 3, 1905 in Buffalo, New York
Died: April 22, 1995

Maggie Kuhn's early childhood was spent in Memphis, Tennessee. In 1916, her family moved to Cleveland, Ohio, where she remained until 1930. Kuhn attended college at Flora Stone Mather College in Cleveland. She credits this college with the beginning of her activism. As part of a sociology class, she visited jails, slums, and sweat shops, where she was made aware of glaring social injustices. While in college, she helped to form a chapter of the League of Women Voters.

In the 1930s and 1940s, Kuhn worked at the Young Women's Christian Association (YWCA) in Cleveland, Philadelphia, and New York. At the YWCA, in the United Services Organization (USO) division, she organized educational and social activities for young women who replaced men in factories while the men were on active duty during World War II. She saw this organization as a bastion for working women. In 1948, the USO division was closed, so she took a job in Boston with the General Alliance for Unitarian and Other Liberal and Christian Women.

She then went to New York City to study social work and theology at Columbia University Teacher's College and Union Theological Seminary. Her parents' health declined during the 1950s and 1960s, so she returned to Cleveland to be closer to them. She supported herself by working for the Presbyterian Church of the United States as the assistant secretary of the Social Education Action Department. As part of her job duties, she edited the journal *Social Progress*, which urged Presbyterians to become more active in social issues. Ironically, among those issues were problems of the elderly. Seven months before her 65th birthday, and after 20 years of employment, the Presbyterian Church asked Kuhn to retire. Her efforts to convince her employers to reverse their decision were unsuccessful.

Kuhn's feelings of hurt and betrayal turned into outrage. She was determined to do something about her forced retirement. Losing her job was a catalyzing moment. She gathered a group of friends together who were suffering the same fate.

Kuhn and her friends decided to organize a group, the Gray Panthers, who would fight against not only ageism, but also the Viet Nam War, sexism, racism, and militarism. The first public meeting of the Gray Panthers was attended by 100 people organized under the motto "Age and Youth in Action"; its members included people of all ages. The organization contended, "Old people and women constitute America's biggest untapped and undervalued human energy source." The Gray Panthers grew from an organization of six members in 1970 to 40,000 at the time of Kuhn's death in 1995. There were as many as 120 local networks in 38 states by 1979, as well as chapters in Tokyo, Dublin, Paris, Stuttgart, Sydney, and Basel. The longevity of the Gray Panthers served as a model for other grassroots organizations that championed housing for the homeless, universal health care, and job training for the unskilled.

During the 1980s, Kuhn spoke out against efforts to cut back social security benefits. She criticized retirement homes for the elderly as "glorified playpens." She fought against the cultural tendency to treat old people like children.

Maggie Kuhn's interest in elder rights was rooted in the belief that human rights and basic justice are essential for society. She viewed all injustices as inextricably linked and focused on peace, presidential elections, poverty, civil liberties, and opposition to war. Kuhn viewed older people as vital human resources in contrast to their portrayal as a social burden.

At age 86, Kuhn wrote her biography, *No Stone Unturned.* It was published in 1991, three years before her death. Kuhn was posthumously inducted into the National Women's Hall of Fame in 1995.

In Her Own Words
"Speak your mind even if your voice shakes."

"At the meeting we discovered we had new freedom as a result of retirement. We had no responsibility to a corporation or organization. We could take risks, speak out. 'With this new freedom we have, let's see what we can do to change the world.'"

"Many, many old people retire from their jobs and retire from life. They have no objective, no purpose. Every one of us needs to have a goal, a passionate purpose…. It's possible to have new roles and a new value system."

"You don't take to the streets until you do your homework."

Resources
Gay, Kathryn, and Martin K. Gay. *Heroes of Conscience: A Biographical Dictionary.* Santa Barbara: ABC-CLIO Inc., 1996. Print.

"Maggie Kuhn." *American Decades.* Ed Judith S. Baughman, et al. Detroit Gale, 1998. *Gale Biography in Context.* Web. 12 Aug. 2011.

"Maggie Kuhn- Answers.com." Web. 12 Aug. 2011. http://www.answers.com/topic/maggie-kuhn/

"Maggie Kuhn." Contemporary Heroes and Heroines. Vol. 2 Gale, 1992. *Gale Biography in Context.* Web. 12 Aug. 2011.

"Maggie Kuhn." *Encyclopedia of World Biography.* Vol 19. Detroit. Gale. 1999. *Gale Biography in Context.* Web. 12 Aug. 2011.

Kuhn, Maggie. *No Stone Unturned, Maggie Kuhn.* New York: Ballentine Books, 1991. Print.

Never let the fear of striking out get in your way.

\- Babe Ruth

Doris Haddock (Granny D.)

Political Activist and Author

At age 90, Doris Haddock, also known as "Granny D," decided to draw attention to the need for campaign reform. She walked 3,200 miles (10 miles a day) from Pasadena, California, to the steps of the capitol in Washington, D.C., to shine a spotlight on the urgency to reform political campaign financing.

Born: January 24, 1910, in Laconia, New Hampshire
Died: March 9, 2010

Doris Haddock was born Ethel Doris Rollins, but she later dropped her first name. She attended Emerson College in Boston, Massachusetts, where she studied acting. Since Emerson students were not allowed to marry, she was expelled from the College for marrying James Haddock after three years of attendance. They had a son and a daughter, eight grandchildren, and 16 great grandchildren.

For 20 years, Haddock worked as a clerk and then as a manager's assistant in a shoe factory in Manchester, New Hampshire. She started hiking as an escape from the tedium of her job. In 1972, the Haddock family moved to Dublin, New Hampshire, where she became active in local government and served on the planning board. She and her husband worked on activist causes, such as stopping the use of hydrogen bombs in Alaska to save an Inuit fishing village in the 1960s. In 1993, her husband died of Alzheimer's disease.

After the death of her husband and daughter, Haddock became more involved in reform causes. She organized petitions for campaign finance reform with thousands of signatures but was not successful in achieving her goals. She knew she needed to do something dramatic, especially since she felt the corporations were taking over and deciding who got elected. She decided to journey across the United States to raise the public's awareness about "the power of big money in American politics." On January 1, 1999, at age 88, Haddock began her walk in Pasadena, California. She walked about 10 miles each day for 14 months.

Throughout her journey, Haddock encountered deserts and blizzards. She had to overcome emphysema and arthritis and was hospitalized for dehydration and pneumonia. Despite these hardships and challenges, Haddock made several speeches along the way. She carried a banner, "Granny D for Campaign Finance Reform," that elicited honks from passing motorists. Politicians came out to pose for pictures with her, and reporters took notes on her speeches and responses to questions. As she walked through 12 states, Haddock attracted national attention. She was greeted by a crowd of 2,200 people, and dozens of members of Congress walked the final miles with her to the capital at the National Mall. Having covered more than 3,200 miles, Haddock arrived in Washington, D.C., on January 29, 2000.

Weeks afterward, Haddock returned to Washington D.C. to continue her protest, and was subsequently arrested inside the Capitol rotunda for illegally protesting. As she was led off by police, bystanders chanted, "Go Granny, Go."

In 2000, Haddock received an honorary degree from Emerson College. She then coauthored two books, *You're Never Too Old to Raise a Little Hell* (2003) and *Granny D: Walking Across America in My Ninetieth*

Year (2001). The material for her first book was taken from a comprehensive journal in which she wrote entries every night. It was Dennis Burke, her travel companion, who encouraged her to publish her writings and assisted her with editing. Barry X. Miller, in the *Library Journal*, described her debut book as "a multilayered memoire ...and a philosophical summation of a life well spent."

When Doris Haddock was 93, after a disappointing 2000 presidential election, she drove over 22,000 miles in a bus through swing states to persuade women to register to vote in the next election. In 2004, she legally changed her name to "Granny D" and ran as a Democratic candidate for a United States Senate seat in New Hampshire against the incumbent Judd Grey. At age 94, she was one of the oldest major party candidates to ever run for the United States Senate. A steadfast advocate for clean elections and campaigns financed by private citizens rather than corporate donations, she accepted only small donations to fund her campaign. Haddock captured about 34% of the vote and lost the election. In 2007, HBO released the documentary, *Run Granny Run* about her Senate campaign. Granny D continued to be active in politics until she died at age 100.

In Her Own Words

"You're never too old to raise a little hell."

"It just infuriates me! I feel we are losing our democracy. The corporations are taking over and deciding who gets elected."

"Our right to alter our government must be used to sweep these halls clean of greedy interests."

Resources

"Doris Haddock," *Contemporary Authors Online*. Detroit: Gale 2010. *Gale Biography in Context*. Web. 12 Aug. 2011.

"Doris Haddock," The Economist [US} 27 Mar. 2010. 83 EU. *Gale Biography in Context*. Web. 12 Aug. 2011.

Haddock, Doris, and Dennis M. Burke. *Granny D: Walking Across America in My Ninetieth Year.* Westminster: Random House P, 2001. Print.

Haddock, Doris, Dennis Burke, and Bill Moyers. *You're Never to Old to Raise a Little Hell.* Westminster: Random House P, 2003. Print.

Hevesi, Dennis. "Doris Haddock, Cross-Country Walker, Is Dead at 100." New York Times 13 Mar. 2010: D8(L) *Gale Biography in Context.* Web. 12 Aug. 2011.

"Great Leaders Lead from a Better Vision of a Possible Future." Commencement Address at New Hampshire College, Amherst, MA. by Doris "Granny D" Haddock. *CommonDreams.org.* CommonDreams, 14 June 2005. Web. 15 Dec. 2013. http://www.commondreams.org/views05/0614-26.htm.

Well behaved women rarely make history.

- Unknown

Mary Harris "Mother" Jones

Labor Organizer

Mary Harris Jones turned personal tragedies into a deep-seated conviction to improve the working conditions of coal miners and children. She was a committed labor and community organizer, as well as an inspiring orator. In 1902, at age 65 or 71(depending on the source), she was proclaimed as, "The most dangerous woman in America."

Born: May 1, 1830, or August 1, 1837, in Cork City, Ireland
Died: November 1, 1930

Mary Harris Jones, the daughter of a Roman Catholic tenant farmer, was born in Ireland. Her family migrated to New York City because her father had to leave their native country after participating in a series of violent uprisings against landlords. Shortly after arriving in the United States, the family moved to Toronto, Canada. In 1857, Jones studied and qualified to become a teacher. In 1860, she left Toronto for Tennessee, where she was hired as a teacher.

In Tennessee, Jones met and married George Jones. He was an iron molder and a part-time organizer for the local Iron Workers Union. Eventually, her husband left the foundry for a full-time position with the Union. Tragically, in the summer of 1867, her husband

and all four of their children, all under the age of 5, died during a yellow fever epidemic.

Under the weight of this personal tragedy, Jones moved to Chicago. There, she supported herself as a seamstress, sewing clothes, draperies, and furniture coverings for wealthy clients. As she barely made enough money to survive, Jones was troubled by her wealthy clients who clearly were oblivious to the poverty that surrounded them. Jones lost her home and business in 1871 in the Great Chicago Fire, which destroyed most of her working-class neighborhood. She became enraged seeing how the city's wealthy citizens were able to recover from the fire, unlike its poor citizens who had no resources to cope with the devastation.

After the fire, Jones joined the Knights of Labor, predecessor of the Workers of the World, a secret organization made up of workers in a variety of professions. She quickly became an active member, organizing and speaking for the organization all over Chicago and thus began a 60-year association with unionism. Ultimately, the Knights of Labor was too conservative and passive for her, so she left the organization and Chicago and later became active as a strike organizer for coal miners throughout the country.

In 1891, Mary Harris Jones unofficially joined the United Mine Workers and, in 1897 became a salaried organizer. She was a flamboyant speaker who was known for her ability to captivate audiences. In addition to meeting with miners, Jones also met with their families to organize wives and children, encouraging them to block entrances to the mines during strikes. She defied judges and other authorities despite harsh restrictions and penalties. She was arrested and jailed at least four times, once spending three months in solitary confinement in a military prison in West Virginia.

Jones also brought attention to the plight of child laborers. In 1903, she organized children who were working in the mines and had them participate in a children's crusade. They marched to the home of President Theodore Roosevelt holding a banner that proclaimed, "We want to go to school and not to the mines." This crusade was described in detail in the 2003 book, *Kids on Strike.*

Although Jones's advocacy is generally admired today, during her lifetime she was viciously attacked with regard to her morals and motivation. In 1902, at age 65 (or 71, depending on the source), she was named by West Virginia's District Attorney, Reese Blizzard, as "the most dangerous woman in America" because of her ability to motivate and organize miners to strike.

In 1920, at age 90, Mother Jones decided to limit her activities. Without a place to live the mine workers opened their homes to her, and she lived with them until her death at either 93 or 100 (depending on the source).

Mother Jones recorded her experiences in the labor movement in a book, *The Autobiography of Mother Jones,* published in 1925. Mother Jones's legacy and work live on in other ways. In 1983, her speeches and writings were published in the book, *Mother Jones Speaks: Speeches and Writings of a Working Class Fighter.* Long after her death, Mother Jones remains "the great grandmother of all agitators." To honor her legacy, the wives and daughters of the striking coal miners assumed the moniker "The Daughters of Mother Jones" in the Pittston Coal Strike in West Virginia and Kentucky in 1989.

Today, *Mother Jones Magazine* covers many of the same social issues that she championed. An elementary school in Adelphi, Maryland is named for her, as is an off-campus service house at Wheeling Jesuit in West Virginia, which requires residents to perform 10 hours of community service each week and participate in community dinners and events in her memory.

In Her Own Words
"Pray for the dead and fight like hell for the living."

"If they want to hang me, let them hang me, but when I am on the scaffold, I'll cry, 'Freedom for the working class'."

Resources

Foner, Philip S., ed. *Mother Jones Speaks: Speeches and Writings of a Working –Class Fighter.* New York: Pathfinder Press, 1983. Print.

Gorn, Elliot J. *Mother Jones: The Most Dangerous Woman in America.* New York: Hill and Wang: Division of Farmer, Straus, and Giroux, 2001. Print.

Jones, Mary Harris. *The Autobiography of Mother Jones.* Chicago: Charles H. Kerr & Co., 1925. Print.

"Mary Harris Jones." *Gale Encyclopedia of U.S. Economic History*, Ed. Thomas Carson and Mary Bonk Detroit Gale 1999 *Gale Biography in Context.* Web. 12 Aug 2011.

*Whoever knocks persistently
ends up by entering.*

- Ali

Clara McBride Hale

Founder, Hale House

Clara Hale was best known for founding Hale House, a home for infants and children who were drug addicted or infected with the human immunodeficiency virus (HIV) at birth. She was a great humanitarian and received many honors.

Born: April 1, 1905, in Elizabeth City, North Carolina
Died: December 18, 1992

Clara Hale was the youngest of four children. Her father died when she was an infant. To provide for her family, her mother took in lodgers and gave them room and board. When Hale was 16, her mother died, leaving her and her siblings orphans. Hale completed high school and married Thomas Hale. The couple moved to New York City from Philadelphia, Pennsylvania. While attending college, her husband opened his own floor waxing business. To supplement their household income, she cleaned theatres.

Thomas Hale died in 1932, and Clara Hale had to support herself and her three small children. To make ends meet, she cleaned houses during the day and theatres at night, leaving her children unsupervised for extended periods. Wanting to spend more time with her children, she opened her own day care business. Many of the children she cared for stayed day and night, seeing their parents who worked as domestics, only on the weekends. In 1940, Hale became a foster parent. Over the next 28 years, she raised 40 foster children, all of whom pursued a college education. In 1968, at age 64, Hale retired from foster care. Soon after her retirement she began another chapter in her life. One day her daughter referred a young drug-addicted mother and baby to Hale for her help. Soon Hale was caring for all the woman's drug-addicted children. By the time the woman returned for her children, Hale had found her calling.

In 1969, Clara Hale began to take in drug-addicted children whose mothers had used drugs during pregnancy. The word spread quickly throughout New York that Hale would care for addicted babies, and soon her home was filled with 22 children. Some had been abandoned, and others were orphaned.

For the first year and a half, Hale, her sons, and daughter provided financial support for the addicted babies by taking as many jobs as necessary to keep the program going. Eventually, they were able to secure a federal grant to renovate a five-story building they named Hale House. In 1970, Percy Sutton, President of the Borough of Manhattan, arranged public funding for Hale House. As a testament to Hale's contributions and value to the community, the singer-songwriter John Lennon, became a financial supporter. Before his death in 1980, he made provisions so the John Lennon Spirit Foundation would continue to fund Hale House.

In 1975, Hale House moved to 122nd Street in Harlem. By 1984, it had a staff of seven college-educated caregivers. Hale's daughter earned a doctorate in child development and became the executive director.

The intervention offered at Hale House is designed for both children and parents. Hale believed in the power of love and positive reinforcement. As the babies went through withdrawal, they were nurtured and cared for but were not given any medications. Addicted mothers were given counseling and assistance to find housing. They were required to participate in an 18-month rehabilitation program and to visit with their children weekly. After successful completion of the program, mothers were reunited with their children. All these services were provided free of charge. After more than 40 years of operation, Hale House has successfully reunited hundreds of families and only 12 children had to be placed for adoption.

Today, Hale House receives referrals from city police, clergy, hospitals, and social workers. It accepts all children, regardless of race, religion, or gender. The children range in age from 10 days to three or four years of age.

Clara Hale was honored repeatedly for her humanitarian work. On February 8, 1985, President Ronald Reagan identified her as a true American hero during his State of the Union Address before Congress. In 1985, she was awarded an Honorary Doctorate of Humane Letters from John Jay College of Criminal Justice. In 1989, she received the Harry S. Truman Award for Public Service. In 1990, she received the Salvation Army's highest award, The Booth Community Service Award.

Clara Hale died in 1992 from stroke complications, after having helped more than 1,000 children

In Her Own Words
"Before I knew it, every pregnant addict in Harlem knew about the crazy lady who would give her baby a home."

"I'd like for it to go down in history that we taught our children to be proud Black American citizens, and that they learned they could do anything, and that they could do it for themselves."

"I'm not an American hero, I'm just someone who loves children."

Resources

Bolden, Tony. *And Not to Dare: the Stories of Ten Black Women.* New York: Scholastic Press, 1968. Print.

"Clara Hale." *Contemporary Heroes and Heroines.* Vol. 3 1998. *Gale Biography in Context.* Web. 12 Aug. 2011.

"Clara Hale." Encyclopedia of World Biography Vol 20. Detroit; Gale, 2000. *Gale Biography in Context.* Web. 12 Aug. 2011.

"Clara Hale." *Encyclopedia of World Biography.* 2004. Encyclopedia. com. Encyclopedia of World Biography, Dec. 2013. Web. 20 May 2012. http://www.enclopedia.com/.

"Clara Hale." *Notable Black American Women.* Gale, 1992, *Gale Biography in Context.* Web. 12 Aug. 2011.

"Clara Hale." *Wikipedia.* Wikipedia, 25 Nov. 2013. Web. 1 Dec. 2013.

Italia, Bob. *Clara Hale: A Mother to Those Who Needed One (Everyone Contributes).* Minneapolis: Abdo Publishers and Co., Inc., 1993. Print.

Lanker, Brian. *I Dream a World. Portraits of Black Women Who Changed America. New York:* Stewart, Tabori, & Chang, 1989. Print.

What lies behind us and what lies before us are small matters compared to what lies within us.

- Ralph Waldo Emerson

Grandma Moses

Artist

When arthritis prevented her from embroidering, at age 76, Anna Mary Robertson began to paint. Her first one-woman show was held in New York City in 1940 when she was 80. Known as Grandma Moses, she is considered to be one of the best 20ᵗʰ century folk artists.

Born: September 7, 1860, in Greenwich, New York
Died: December 13, 1961

Grandma Moses was born Anna Mary Robertson, the third of 10 children. She reportedly had a happy childhood and loved to draw cheerful colorful scenes. Her father enjoyed his children's drawings and bought them large sheets of blank newsprint so they could draw. Moses worked hard on the family farm. Because of her family's financial difficulties, she had no winter clothing, so she attended school only in the summer. At age 12, Moses stopped attending her one-room school house and began working in neighboring homes as a domestic.

In 1887, Moses married a farm worker, Thomas S. Moses, and they settled on a farm in Virginia. They had 10 children, five of whom died at birth. In 1907, the family moved to Eagle Bridge, New York, where Moses lived for the rest of her life. It was at the Eagle Bridge farm where she created her first painting. Moses had run out of wall paper for the parlor, so she completed the project by placing a blank sheet of paper on the wall and painting a scene on it. Today, that first painting hangs in the Bennington Museum in Bennington, Vermont.

In 1927, her husband died. Eventually, farming became too difficult for Moses, so her son and daughter took over the farm. To pass the time, Moses took up embroidery. In her 70s, Moses took up painting and abandoned embroidery because of arthritis.

Grandma Moses's early work was based on scenes and prints such as those by Currier and Ives. Eventually, she started creating original pieces based on her memories of 19th century farm life through which she developed her unique folk style. Sometimes she painted herself into the scenes as she looked as a child. Moses also painted some historical pictures featuring her ancestors, some of whom were dressed in 18th century rural costumes.

In 1938, Louis Caldor (an engineer and art collector) discovered Moses's paintings in a drug store window, in Hoosick Falls, New York. After initially purchasing four paintings, he later bought all of Moses's other paintings. In 1939, three of these paintings were exhibited in the Contemporary Unknown Painters Show at New York's Museum of Modern Art. In 1939, an art dealer exhibited some of her work at the Gallerie Saint-Etienne in New York City. In 1940, at age 80, Moses held her first one-woman show in New York exhibiting 35 of her paintings which brought her national and international recognition. In 1942, at age 82, Moses held her second one-woman show in New York.

By 1943, there was an overwhelming demand for Moses's nostalgic paintings. Some of her most popular paintings were: "The Old Oaken Bucket," "Over the River to Grandma's House," "Sugaring Off," and "Catching the Turkey." In 1946, her painting, "The Old Checkered Inn in Summer" was featured in the background of a national advertising campaign for DuBarry Cosmetics, and her paintings were regularly reproduced on Hallmark greeting cards. She painted "Fourth of July" in honor of President Eisenhower and it still hangs in the White House today. Altogether Grandma Moses painted more than 1,000 canvases in three decades.

In 1949, President Harry Truman presented Grandma Moses with the Woman's National Press Club Trophy Award for outstanding accomplishment in art. At age 91, she appeared on the television program, *See It Now*, hosted by Edward R. Murrow. At age 92, Moses published her autobiography, *Grandma Moses, My Life's History*. On her 100th birthday, then New York Governor Nelson Rockefeller proclaimed the day Grandma Moses Day in her honor. She also received many other awards and honorary doctorates.

In the last year of her life, she painted 25 more canvases, two of which, "Rainbow" and "White Birches," are considered to be among her finest works. At age 100, Moses illustrated an edition of *The Night Before Christmas* by Clement Moore. She painted "Sugaring Off" in 1961. It was sold for $1.2 million in November 2006.

In Her Own Words

"I look back on my life, like a good day's work... I was happy and contented. I knew nothing better and made the best out of what life offered. And life is what we make it, always has been, always will be."

"I get an inspiration and start painting; then I forget everything, everything except how things used to be and how to paint it so people will know how we used to live."

Resources

"Anna (Grandma) Moses." *Contemporary Women Artists*. Gale, 1999. *Gale Biography in Context*. Web. 12 Aug. 2011.

Biracee, Tom. *Grandma Moses*. New York: Chelsea House, 1989. Print.

"Grandma Moses." *Contemporary Heroes and Heroines.* Vol. 2. Gale, 1992. *Gale Biography in Context.* Web. 12 Aug. 2011.

"Grandma Moses Biography." *Encyclopedia of World Biography Online.* Encyclopedia of World Biography. Web. 1 Dec. 2013.

"Grandma Moses." *Encyclopedia of World Biography.* Detroit. Gale, 1998. *Gale Biography in Context.* Web. 12 Aug. 2011.

"Grandma Moses." *Gale Encyclopedia of Biography Online.* Gale Encyclopedia of Biography. Web. 1 Dec. 2013.

Kallir, Jane. *Grandma Moses in 21st Century.* Alexandria: Art Services International, 2001. Print.

If you do not change direction you may end up where you are heading.

\- Lao Tzu

Edith Hamilton

Author, Greatest Woman Classicist

At age 63, in 1930, Edith Hamilton published The Greek Way, *the first of many acclaimed books devoted to Greek and Roman culture. As a result of her scholarship, she received many awards, including several honorary doctorates, and was proclaimed an honorary citizen of Athens, Greece.*

Born: August 12, 1867, in Dresden, Germany
Died: May 31, 1963

The daughter of Gertrude and Montgomery Hamilton, Edith Hamilton was born in Dresden, Germany, during a visit with her mother's family. Hamilton's family was wealthy and interested in intellectual pursuits. Her father and mother were voracious readers; her father taught her Latin at age seven and Greek at age eight. Hamilton's mother taught her French, and her servants taught her German. Like her mother and father, she also became an avid reader.

Hamilton was determined to be educated. Along with her three sisters, at age 16, she attended school for the first time at Ms. Porter's School in Farmington, Connecticut. Since the school didn't require any particular courses and students could study whatever they liked, Hamilton later reported that she "...didn't learn anything." Despite the objections of Ms. Porter and her family, Hamilton's desire for knowledge led her to attend Bryn Mawr College where she majored in the classics and finished in two years with a master's of arts in 1894.

While at Bryn Mawr, Hamilton was awarded the European Fellowship. This award was given to the most outstanding woman in the graduating class and enabled the recipient to study abroad for a year. In 1895, she and her sister Alice, who had recently graduated as a physician, chose the University of Leipzig in Germany where they were the University's first female students. Hamilton was very dissatisfied with the education she received there. Although she was able to take Greek and Latin courses, the emphasis was only on grammar and not on an understanding of the materials. Disenchanted, she and Alice left Leipzig. Hamilton then enrolled in courses at the University of Munich, where she again had the distinction of being the first female student. Her admission to the University caused such an uproar that she was forced to sit alone on the lecturer's platform to avoid "contaminating" the male students. This experience of isolation did not discourage her. She felt the professors were more knowledgeable and the courses were more interesting than her previous experiences.

Hamilton would have remained at the University of Munich to complete her doctoral degree, but her father suffered financial difficulties. Fortunately, Ms. M. Carey Thomas offered her a position as the first head mistress of the Bryn Mawr Preparatory School in Baltimore, Maryland. In 1896, at age 29, she arrived at the preparatory school. She faced the challenges of learning a job for which she had no experience and convincing the parents of her students that their daughters needed a true education. Although Hamilton was apprehensive at first, she persevered and eventually gained a reputation as a gifted teacher. She held her students to high academic standards, yet instilled in them a love of learning. Hamilton modeled her theories of education on the educational philosophy of the ancient Greeks, who emphasized the importance of developing each student's individual talents.

In 1922, after 26 years as head mistress, Hamilton resigned to become a full-time writer. She divided her time between two cities, spending summers in Seawall, Maine, and winters in New York City. At a gathering in her New York apartment, she was asked to write an article for *Theatre Arts Monthly* on Greek tragedies. At first she refused the invitation, but was finally persuaded to write the piece. After the article was favorably reviewed, she submitted several other articles that eventually became the basis of her first book, *The Greek Way*. The book, published in 1930, when Hamilton was 63, captured the spirit of the ancient Greeks and applied their philosophy to contemporary society. Following the critical acclaim of her first book, Hamilton published *The Roman Way* in 1932, and Mythology: *Timeless Tales of Gods and Heroes* in 1942. Both books are now considered classics for high school and university students, and *Mythology* remains the premier introductory text. In her 90s, Hamilton continued to add to her critically acclaimed body of work, culminating in the publication of *The Echo of Greece*, the sequel to *The Greek Way*, and *The Age of Heroes: An Introduction to Greek Mythology*, and other books that were published posthumously.

Edith Hamilton received many honors and awards, including the National Achievement and the Constant Lindsay Skinner Award for Literature. She also received honorary doctorates from the University of Rochester, the University of Pennsylvania, Yale University, and was elected as a member of The National Institute of Arts and Letters. She was even invited to Athens in 1957 where then King Paul of Greece gave her the Gold Cross of the Legion of Benefaction and made her an honorary citizen of the city.

Hamilton is still considered the greatest woman classicist who, as the *New York Times* described, "brought into clear and brilliant focus the Golden Age of Greek life and thought...with Homeric power and simplicity in her style of writing."

In Her Own Words

"Ideals have tremendous power. When ideals are low they fade out and are forgotten; Great ideals have had power of persistent life."

Resources

Brown, John Mason. *Seeing More Things.* New York: Whittlesey House, 1948. Print.

"Edith Hamilton." *Contemporary Authors Online.* Detroit. Gale. 2000. *Gale Biography in Context.* Web. 12 Aug. 2011.

"Hamilton, Edith (1867-1963)." *Encyclopedia of World Biography.*" Detroit. Gale. 1998 *Gale Biography in Context.* Web. 12 Aug. 2011.

Reed, Doris F. *Edith Hamilton: an Intimate Portrait.* New York: Norton and Co, 1967. Print.

Stoddard, Hope. *Famous American Women.* New York: Crowell, 1970. Print.

"UNH Classics Program Pays Tribute to Edith Hamilton at Rouman Lecture April 21." States News Service 19 Apr. 2010. *Gale Biography in Context.* Web. 12 Aug. 2011.

Success is not final, failure is not fatal; it is the courage to continue that counts.

\- Winston Churchill

Harlan David Sanders

Restaurateur, Entrepreneur

Harlan David Sanders, a Midwestern farm boy and grade school dropout, never let his many failures define him. He was resilient and had many careers. At the time in his life when he was subsisting on Social Security checks and meager savings, he founded the restaurant chain Kentucky Fried Chicken, now known as KFC.

Born: September 9, 1890, Henryville, Indiana
Died: December 16, 1980

Harlan David Sanders was born in Henryville, Indiana. His father, a butcher, died when he was five. Because his mother had to work long hours at a cannery factory to support the family and Harlan Sanders was the oldest of the three Sanders children; his job was to cook for the family. He held his first job outside the home when he was 10 years old at a nearby farm, where he further developed his cooking skills. Around that time, Sanders's mother remarried and moved with her children to Greenville, Indiana, with her new husband.

Accounts differ as to why Sanders left his new home when he was 12 years old. In the following years, he worked a succession of jobs: a farmhand, an insurance salesman, a secretary of a chamber of commerce, and a streetcar conductor. In 1906, he enlisted in the U.S. Army and served a year in Cuba. After his discharge, he married Josephine King and they had 3 children. They divorced in 1947.

Also, Sanders was hired as a "railroad man" with the Illinois Central Railroad. While working at this job, he earned a law degree by taking a correspondence course from Southern University. Subsequently he practiced law from 1915 to the early 1920s working in the Justice of the Peace courts in Little Rock, Arkansas.

After practicing law, he moved to Corbin, Kentucky, and opened a gas station in 1929. When customers asked where they could get something to eat, he got the idea to open a restaurant that specialized in Southern cooking. He eventually expanded his business to a motel complex across the street and took an eight-week course in hotel restaurant management from Cornell University to better manage his business. In 1937, his café became so popular that it came to the attention of Governor Ruby Laffoon, who honored Sanders with the title of honorary Kentucky colonel. Despite this recognition, Sanders next ventures were unsuccessful.

Over the next nine years, Sanders developed his secret method of cooking chicken. Knowing that his customers couldn't wait the typical 45 minutes for chicken to cook, he devised a method using a pressure cooker - a new invention at the time- to shorten the cooking process to nine minutes.

When Sanders was once again given the title of honorary Kentucky colonel in 1949, he began dressing in the style of an old southern gentleman, the image he is now known by. In the same year he married Claudia Ledington, a company employee.

By the early 1950s, Sanders thought that his chicken recipe had been perfected enough to franchise. He sold his "11 herbs and spices" recipe to restaurant owners for five cents per chicken. This arrangement was an early version of his Kentucky Fried Chicken franchise. Pete Harmon, a restaurateur from Salt Lake City, Utah, became his first franchisee and helped him with marketing strategies.

When a highway was planned to bypass Corbin, the value of Sanders's property declined dramatically. Due to the decline in value, he auctioned off the property for $75,000 to pay his debts. Left solely dependent on Social Security benefits and meager savings, at age 66, he decided to sell his secret fried chicken recipe to restaurants. He marketed his chicken as "Colonel Sanders's Recipe Kentucky Fried Chicken." He took his cooking equipment to selected restaurants, where he prepared a sample of his chicken. His wife, Claudia, often accompanied him, dressed to complement his outfit.

Within three years, he had established dozens of Kentucky Fried Chicken franchises that sold chicken cooked with his recipe throughout the Midwest. By 1960, he had 400 such franchises. By 1963, he made $300,000 a year before taxes. When Colonel Sanders sold the entire franchise in 1964, it was valued at $2 million. In addition, he received a $40,000 lifetime salary per year which was later raised to $75,000.

Sanders's first restaurant was named a Kentucky historical landmark in 1972. At age 84, he wrote his autobiography, *Life as I Have Known It Has Been Finger-Lickin' Good.* Colonel Sanders remained an ambassador for the company he founded, at age 90, traveling more than 250,000 miles each year.

Today, Colonel Sanders's chicken is still famous for being "finger-lickin' good," and his recipe remains a trade secret. His company, now simply known as KFC, stands as a testament to his success.

In His Own Words
"Life as I Have Known It Has Been Finger-Lickin Good" from the book of the same name.

Resources

"Colonel Sanders." Authors Online. Contemporary Authors Online. Detroit. *Gale Biography in Context.* Web. 12 Aug. 2011.

"Colonel Sanders." *Encyclopedia.com.* Encyclopedia, 2004. Web. 1 Dec. 2013.

"Colonel Sanders." Encyclopedia of World Biography. Vol. 19. Detroit: Gale, 1999. *Gale Biography in Context.* Web. 12 Aug. 2011.

Cooksey, Gloria. "Colonel Sanders." *Scribner Encyclopedia of American Lives, Thematic Series: Sports Figures.* Ed. Arnold Markoe and Kenneth T. Jackson. New York: Charles Scribner's Sons, 2003. *Gale Biography in Context.* Web. 12 Aug. 2011.

Sanders, Colonel Harlan. *Life as I Have Known It Has Been Finger-Lickin' Good.* Carol Stream: Creation House, 1974. Print.

Notables

Everybody dies but not everybody lives.

- Unknown

Peter Oakley

Social Media Star

In 2006, at age 79, Peter Oakley became a YouTube media star. His style of storytelling has captivated audiences and led to tremendous popularity of his personal Internet video casting.

Born: August 20, 1927, Leicester, England

In August 2006, at age 79, Peter Oakley made his YouTube debut with a series of 5-to-10 minute autobiographical videos titled, *Telling It All*. In his videos, Oakley reveals, under the alias Geriatric 1927, that he served as a radar mechanic during World War II, that he loves motorcycles, and that he lives alone as a widower and pensioner.

Oakley was an immediate sensation with the YouTube community. A week after his debut, he became the most subscribed user on YouTube. By November, 2006, he had more than 30,000 subscribers. In response to his growing popularity, Oakley was interviewed on February 16, 2007, on British Broadcasting Corporation's *The Money Program*. By April 2009, Oakley had released more than 200 videos.

Peter Oakley has been dubbed "the coolest old dude alive," by the You Tube community for his use of personal Internet video casting and has been praised for his style of storytelling. He begins his videos with his catchphrase, "Hello, YouTubers," or "Good evening, YouTubers." He closes by thanking his viewers and gently saying "Good-bye." Because of his Internet presence, other senior citizens are sharing their life experiences and beginning to post video logs.

Resources

Ask Geriatric. The Official 1927 Geriatric 1927 Website. Web. 1 Dec. 2013. http://www.youtube.com/watch?v=s73BHr8R6fg.

"Pensioner Tops Web Video Clips." *The Guardian OnLine.* The Guardian, 13 Aug. 2006. Web. 1 Dec. 2013.

"Peter Oakley." *Wikipedia.org.* Wikipedia, 24 Nov. 2013. Web. 1 Dec. 2013.

"Telling It All 20." *YouTube.* YouTube, 18 Sept. 2006. Web. 1 Dec. 2013.

The idea is to die young as late as possible.

\- www.thescientist.com

The Zimmers Group

Rock Stars

The musical group, The Zimmers, was formed in 2007 with arguably the oldest members in the world. The lead singer was 90, and the other members ranged in age from 71 to 102. They released their version of the Who's hit, "My Generation," and it reached 26 on the singles chart in the United Kingdom.

Formed: in 2007 in England

On May 27, 2007, the Zimmers, a 40-member band, was created for a British Broadcasting Corporation (BBC) television documentary. The idea originated with Tim Samuels after he made a documentary about the disenfranchisement of the elderly and their feelings of isolation and loneliness. The Zimmers took their name from the British term for a device to help people walk (the Zimmer Frame). This band is believed to have the oldest members of any band in the world. In 2007, the year they formed, the youngest member was 71 years old, the oldest member was 102 and the lead singer, Alf, was 90.

The Zimmers's music is intended to express the feelings of isolation and imprisonment suffered by the elderly. This sentiment was expressed in the group's first single, My Generation, which reached number 26 on the United Kingdom's singles chart. On July 13,

2007, the Zimmers announced their second single, "Fire Starter." In September 2008, the band released its first full-length album, "Lust for Life."

Alf Caretta, the group's former lead singer, died on June 29, 2010, at age 93. Even with this loss, the group still continues to perform and appeared on Britain's Got Talent singing The Beastie Boys' hit, (You Gotta) Fight for Your Right (To Party!).

In Their Own Words

"Let them see that older people can do things. Don't put us in the dust bin yet." The Zimmers

Resources

Baker, Luke. "British Geriatrics Take to the Rock Star Life." *Reuters Edition Online.* Reuters Edition, 30 May 2007. Web. 1 Dec. 2013.

"Power to the People: The Great Granny Chart Invasion." *YouTube.* YouTube. 26 March 2012. Web. 1 Dec. 2013.

"Power to the People- a three part series of mischievous documentaries." *BBC News, BBC Two.* BBC News, BBC Two, 2 May 2007. Web. 01 Dec. 2013.

Samuels, Tim. "What the Zimmers did next." *BBC News Magazine.* BBC News Magazine, 9 Oct. 2008. Web. 1 Dec. 2013.

"Rock Elders Aim for Chart Success." *BBC News Online.* BBC News, 13 Apr. 2007. Web. 1 Dec. 2013.

When it comes to the future, there are three kinds of people: those who let it happen, those who make it happen, and those who wondered what happened.

\- Carol Christensen

Fauja Singh

Marathon Runner

At age 89, Fauja Singh ran his first marathon in London. At age 100, he became the oldest person ever to complete a marathon finishing the Toronto marathon in eight hours in 2011.

Born April 1, 1911, in India

Fauja Singh was a farmer who developed his jogging skills on a farm in Punjab, India. After his wife's death, he moved to England at age 81 to live with his son. Seeing the unhealthy habits of most people his age in England, he decided to do something different. That decision, coupled with the boredom he was experiencing, led him to rediscover jogging. His marathon debut was at the London Marathon when he was 89. He completed this first run in 6 hours and 54 minutes. He continued to compete and eventually improved his time by more than an hour. By age 94, he had run seven marathons- five in London, one in Toronto, and one in New York. He also has run countless half-marathons between these events and is a member of the world's oldest marathon team in Edinburgh, Scotland. Singh is a super star. He signed an endorsement contract with Adidas (the sports company) and is part of their "Nothing Is Impossible" campaign. He has used his status to help raise thousands of dollars for BLISS, a charity dedicated to caring for premature infants.

He continues his training regimen which includes a daily eight-mile walk and run. He also meditates, avoids smoking and drinking, smiles often, and eats plenty of ginger curry.

In His Own Words

"The first 20 miles are not difficult. As for the last six miles, I run while talking to God."

Resources

"Fauja Singh." *Wikipedia.org.* Wikipedia, 1 Nov. 2013. Web. 1 Dec. 2013.

"100-year old Marathoner Finishes Toronto Race." *Associated Press.* Associated Press, 16 Oct. 2011. Web. 1 Dec. 2013. http://www.nbc-sports.com/other-sports/100-year-old-marathoner-finishes-Toronto-race.com/.

"101-Year-Old Man Finishes Toronto Marathon." *National Public Radio.* NATL. Public Radio, 17 Oct. 2011. Web. 1 Dec. 2013.

"101-Year-Old 'Turbaned Tornado' Retires from Running." *National Public Radio.* NATL. Public Radio, 25 Feb. 2013. Web. 1 Dec. 2013.

Websites:

http://fateh.sikhnet.com/Sikhhnet/Register.nsf/Files/Wallpaper4/$file

http://news.bbc.co.uk/sport2/hi/funny_old_game/4631111.stm

http://fateh.sikhnet.com

www.sikhiwiki.org/index.php/Fauja_Singh

The secret of success is constancy of purpose.

- Benjamin Disraeli

William Hawkins

Artist

William Hawkins was in his 80s before he became widely recognized as an artist. Although not formally trained, his paintings are now found in private collections and museums throughout the United States.

Born: 1895 in rural Kentucky
Died: 1990

William Hawkins was born in rural Kentucky and began creating art as a boy. At age 26, he moved to Columbus, Ohio, where he began working at a variety of jobs that continued throughout his life. He had a wealth of practical knowledge, even though his formal education ended in the third grade. In his early paintings, his rural background influenced his art, as seen in his many paintings of animals. His life in Columbus influenced his later work as evidenced by his cityscapes.

The materials Hawkins used were as unique as his paintings- cans of leftover paint and discarded old boards. He worked with a single brush, using it until it was worn and then painting with the handle. He began his career painting mostly in black, white, and gray, and later expanded his pallet to include other colors. Hawkins incorporated found objects in his art, painted his frames, and signed his work with a bold signature.

Hawkins became widely known as an artist in his 80s. In 1982, at age 87, one of his pieces was entered in the Ohio State Fair where he won first place in the amateur division. Since that initial success, his work has become part of many museum collections throughout the United States. Hawkins continued to work until his death at age 94. The first retrospective of his work was held posthumously in 1997 at the Museum of Folk Art in New York City.

In His Own Words

"Now everyone today, they got to go to school to draw! I've been drawing all my life...anything I see just come to me."

"There are a million artists out there and I try to be the greatest of them."

Resources

Karlins, N.F. "Williams Hawkins: Outsider, Now Very In." *artnet. com/magazine.* Artnet Magazine, 30 Oct. 1997. Web. 21 Feb. 2010.

Rexer, Lyle. *How to Look at Outsider Art.* New York: Abrams, Inc. P, 2005. Print.

"William Hawkins (1895-1990) American Folk Art." *KenyGalleries. com.* Keny Galleries, 28 Apr. 2009. Web. 1 Dec. 2013.

Nothing is impossible. The word itself says I'm possible.

\- Audrey Hepburn

The Rusty Pistols: Gary Richardson, Lee Hubbard, and Bud Fry

Basketball Champs

Competitive basketball is traditionally a game for youth, but there are competitive basketball tournaments for older players. Gary Richardson, Lee Hubbard, and Bud Fry, known as the Rusty Pistols, have challenged the traditional attitudes about athleticism and aging by competing and winning tournaments in the 65 plus division.

Gary Richardson and Bud Fry began playing basketball together at Louisiana Tech in 1956. Richardson led the team in rebounding; Fry was known for his great shooting. Because of their prowess, Louisiana Tech was one of the best small-school collegiate basketball programs in the United States. Now Fry runs a plastic molding company in Longview, Texas, and Richardson coordinates a technology program at the University of Houston. Having remained in contact after college, they reunited in 1993 to play basketball when Richardson was 55 and Fry was 56. They competed in an age division called, Older than Dirt, and came up with the team name Rusty Pistols. When Lee Hubbard, from Temple, Texas, joined them, they began to collect gold medals in tournaments all over Texas.

The Rusty Pistols have competed in national and international tournaments. In 2003, they won a gold medal in the 65 plus division at the National Senior Games in Virginia. Also, the Rusty Pistols played in the international basketball competition known as FIMBA. FIMBA's age categories for males are from 35 to 75 years of age. In 2009, in Prague, Czech Republic, Richardson and Fry helped the Men's Basketball Team (70 year old division) win a gold medal at the FIMBA Maxi Basketball Championships. The team beat Russia in the title game of this competition. Despite health challenges, the Rusty Pistols continue to play basketball.

In Their Own Words

"Everyone's going to die sometime. You can either do it sitting in a rocking chair or go out doing what you love." - Gary Richardson

Resources

Godwin, Jordan. "Don't Call This Pistol Old- Just Old-School." *Houston Chronicle* 14 July 2009: C1+. Print.

Godwin, Jordan. "Over-70 Hoops: These Rusty Pistols Can Still Shoot." *Chron.com*. Chron, 14 July 2009. Web. 01 Dec. 2013.

Conclusion

We have provided examples of people who have achieved extraordinary success for the first time after age 60. It has often been said, "Do something significant by age 25, or you never will." Clearly, the 25 individuals described in our book did not adhere to this belief. Our hope in writing this book is that it will inspire people of all ages to pursue their goals, never give up, and realize that success can happen at any stage of life.

Karen L. Pepkin
Wendell C. Taylor

*Life should have a mission and
not be an intermission.*
- Unknown

*You miss 100% of the
shots you don't take.*
- Wayne Gretzky

Karen L. Pepkin is an educational consultant/trainer who has published resources in her field as well as two cookbooks. Wendell C. Taylor is a social psychologist with training in public health. As a professor in public health, he is widely published in numerous scholarly journals. Together, they are coauthors of two books (*Senior Wonders: People Who Achieved Their Dreams After Age 60* and *Booster Breaks: Improving Employee Health One Break at a Time*).

In their sixties, the authors understand the frustration and disappointment of not achieving goals or dreams. They often hear from friends, family, and others that the most painful regrets are not about the mistakes they made but about things never tried, ambitions never pursued, or roads never taken. *Senior Wonders* is the authors' combined effort to address this dissatisfaction and inspire people of all ages not to give up on their dreams.

Printed in Great Britain
by Amazon

38473599R00076